JUST HAVE

MW01200861

H°W DOES THIS B°°K WORK ?

1. Y°U AND Y°UR PARTNER HAVE T° FILL °UT ALL THE BLANK C°UPONS.
(BE DIRTY, YOU CAN !)

2. OPEN THE B°°K RAND°MLY AND LET Y°U GO!!!

3. LEAVE A NICE REVIEW FOR OTHER C°STUMERS.
WE ALWAYS WANT T° KN°W Y°UR °PINION !

ONE TICKET VALID FOR

STRIP TEASE

ONE TICKET VALID FOR

ONE TICKET VALID FOR

_____

ONE TICKET VALID FOR

ICE CUBES...

ONE TICKET VALID FOR

_____

ONE TICKET VALID FOR

_____

ONE TICKET VALID FOR

DESSERT

+

FULL BODY MASSAGE

ONE TICKET VALID FOR

ONE TICKET VALID FOR

SEND NAUGHTY
NOTES AND PHOTO

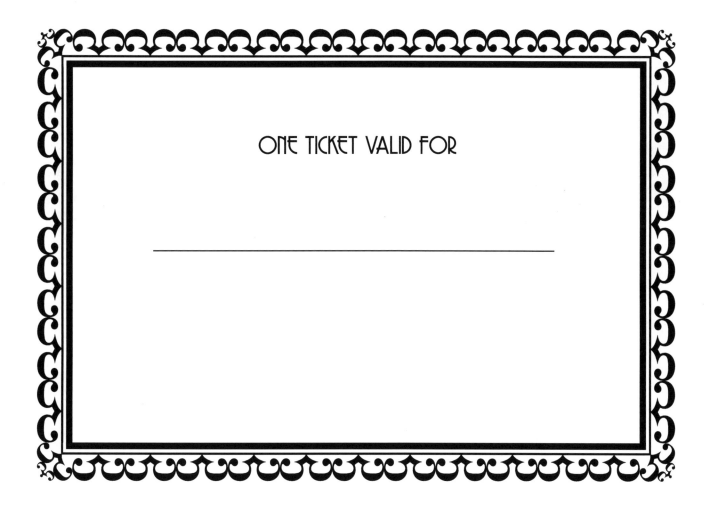

ONE TICKET VALID FOR

_____

ONE TICKET VALID FOR

WHATEVER SHE DECIDES

ONE TICKET VALID FOR

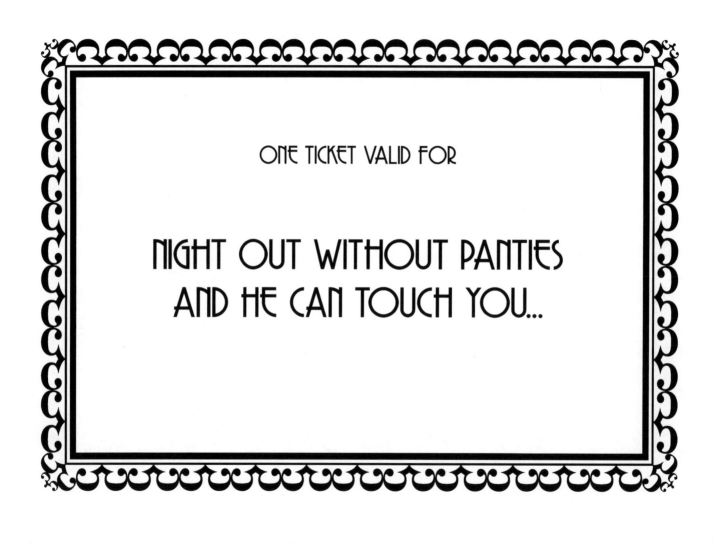

ONE TICKET VALID FOR

_____

ONE TICKET VALID FOR

ONE TICKET VALID FOR

ONE TICKET VALID FOR

WHATEVER SHE DECIDES

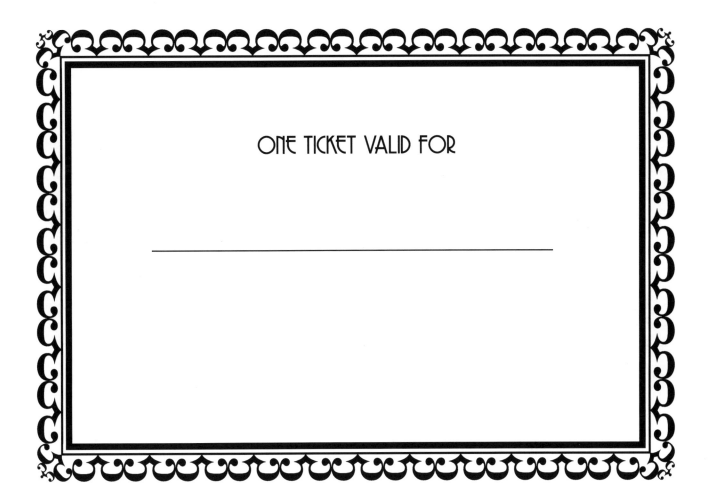

ONE TICKET VALID FOR

_____

ONE TICKET VALID FOR

WHIPPED CREAM

ONE TICKET VALID FOR

ONE TICKET VALID FOR

HEAVY PETTING IN DISCO

ONE TICKET VALID FOR

_____

ONE TICKET VALID FOR

WILD CARD

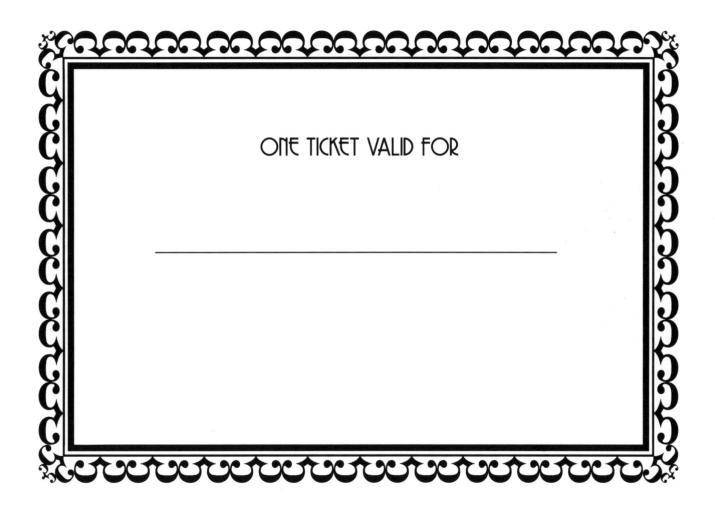

ONE TICKET VALID FOR

_____

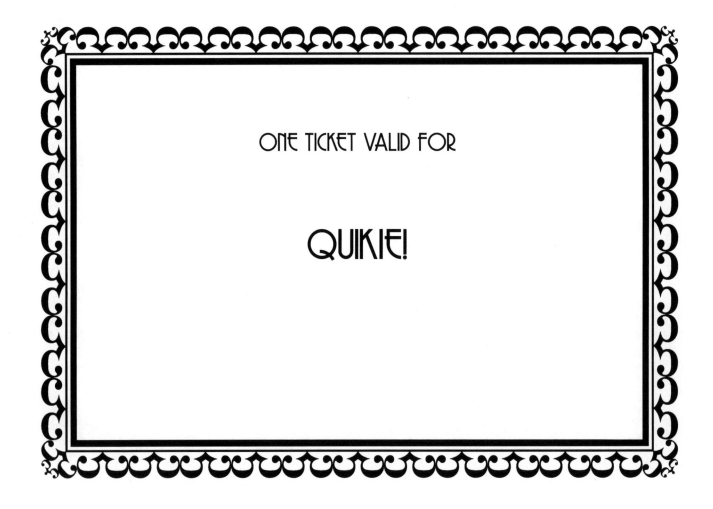

ONE TICKET VALID FOR

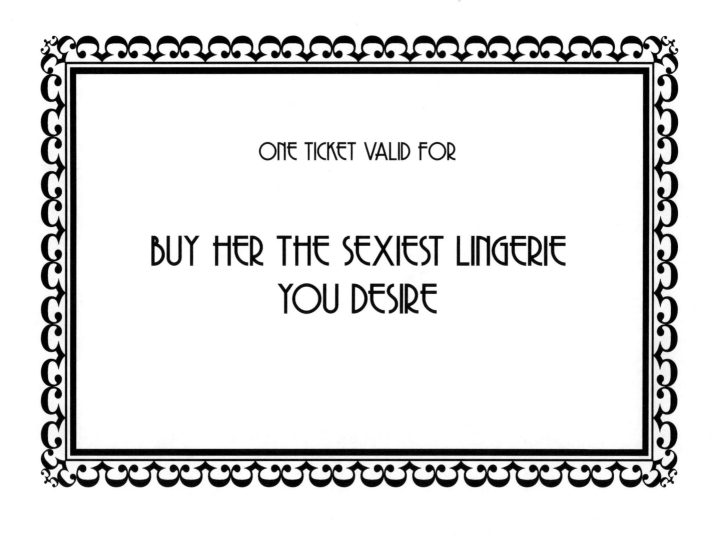

ONE TICKET VALID FOR

BUY HER THE SEXIEST LINGERIE
YOU DESIRE

ONE TICKET VALID FOR

_____

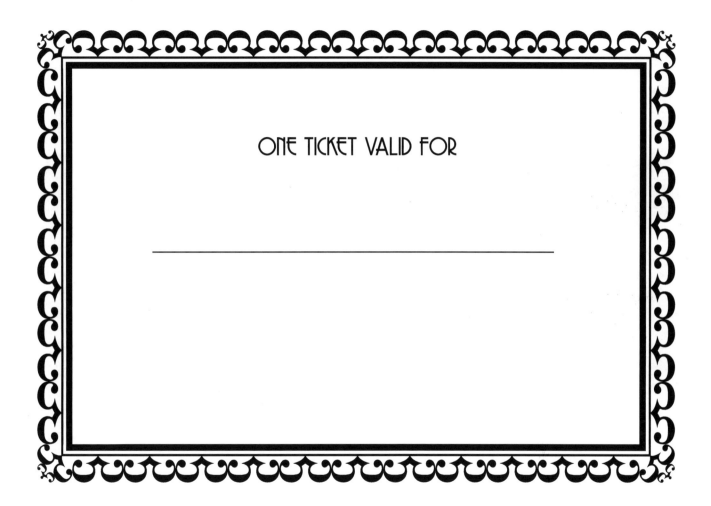

ONE TICKET VALID FOR

_____

ONE TICKET VALID FOR

SPANK TIME!

ONE TICKET VALID FOR

_____

ONE TICKET VALID FOR

DRESS UP TIME SEX

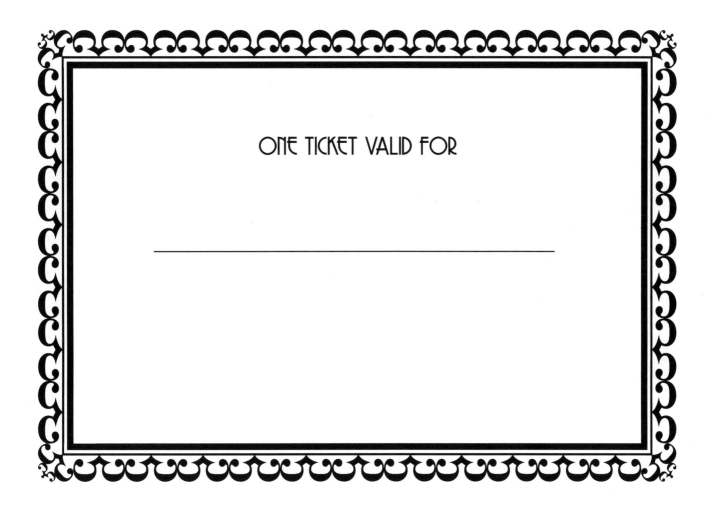

ONE TICKET VALID FOR

_____

ONE TICKET VALID FOR

_____

ONE TICKET VALID FOR

DRUNK SEX

ONE TICKET VALID FOR

_____

ONE TICKET VALID FOR

_____

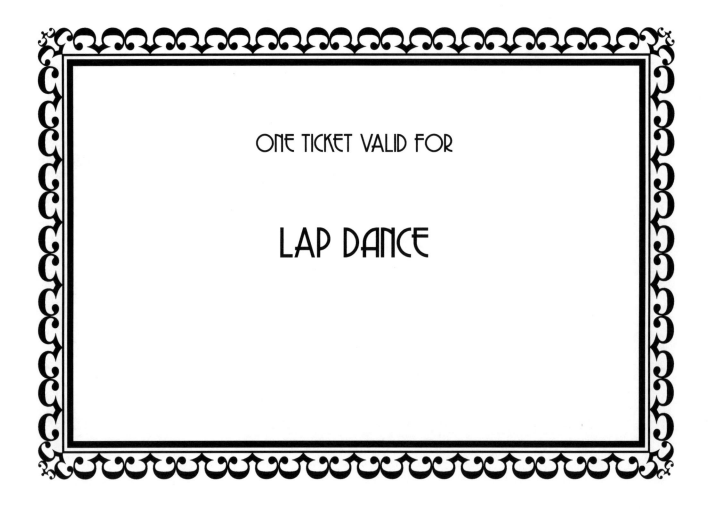

ONE TICKET VALID FOR

LAP DANCE

ONE TICKET VALID FOR

_____

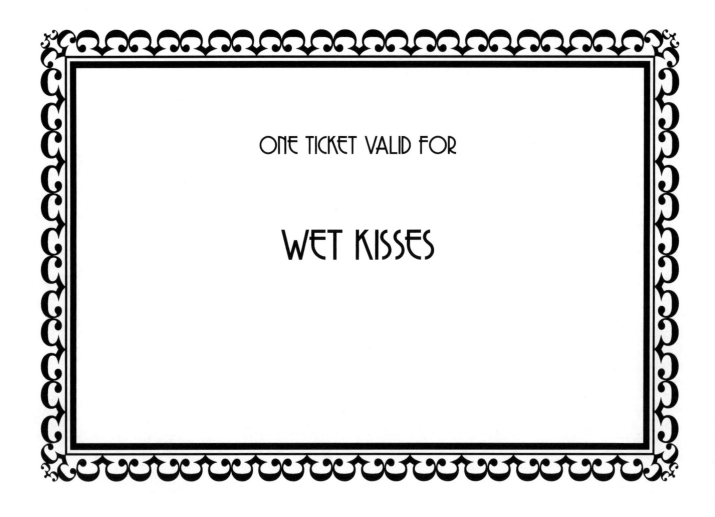

ONE TICKET VALID FOR

WET KISSES

ONE TICKET VALID FOR

_____

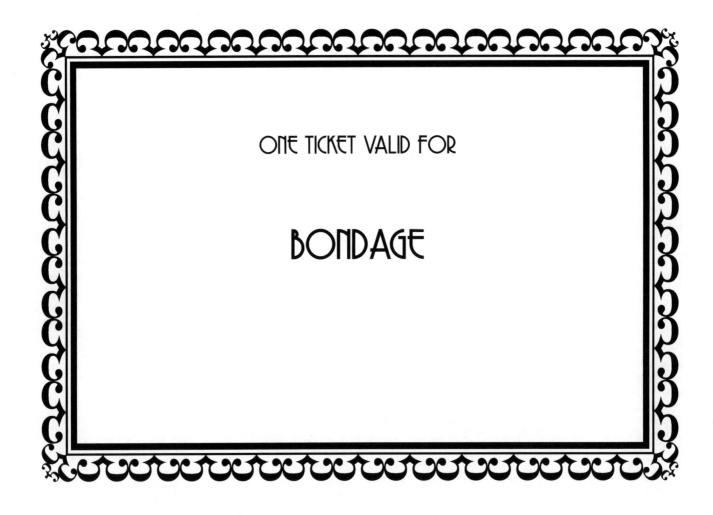

ONE TICKET VALID FOR

BONDAGE

ONE TICKET VALID FOR

_____

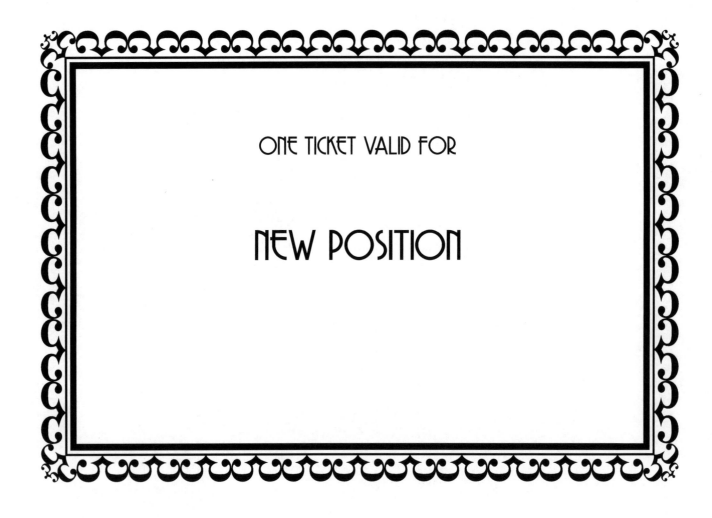

ONE TICKET VALID FOR

NEW POSITION

ONE TICKET VALID FOR

_____

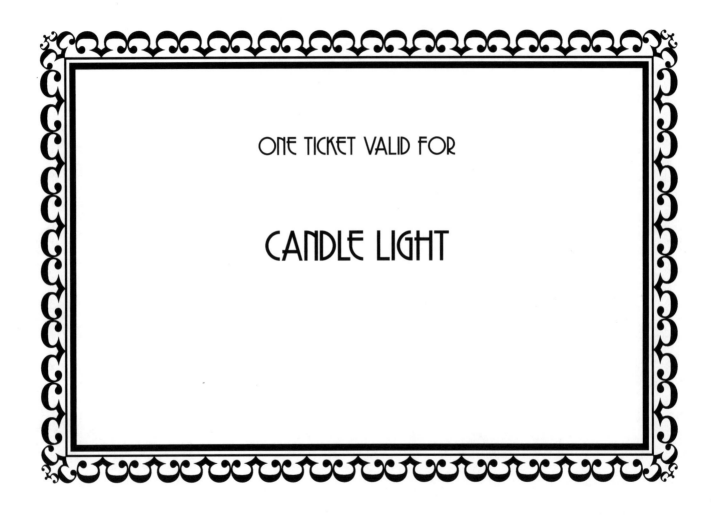

ONE TICKET VALID FOR

CANDLE LIGHT

ONE TICKET VALID FOR

_____

ONE TICKET VALID FOR

CLOSE THE LIPS AND SUCK IT

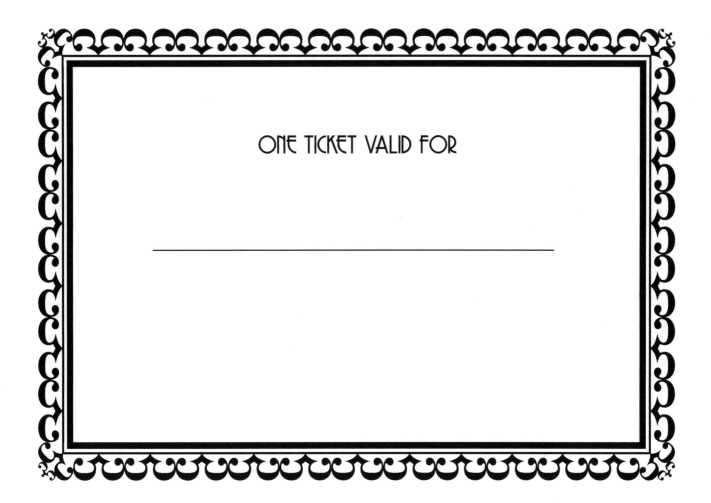

ONE TICKET VALID FOR

_____

ONE TICKET VALID FOR

TAKE HER A PRESENT
AND LICK HER WIDELY

ONE TICKET VALID FOR

_____

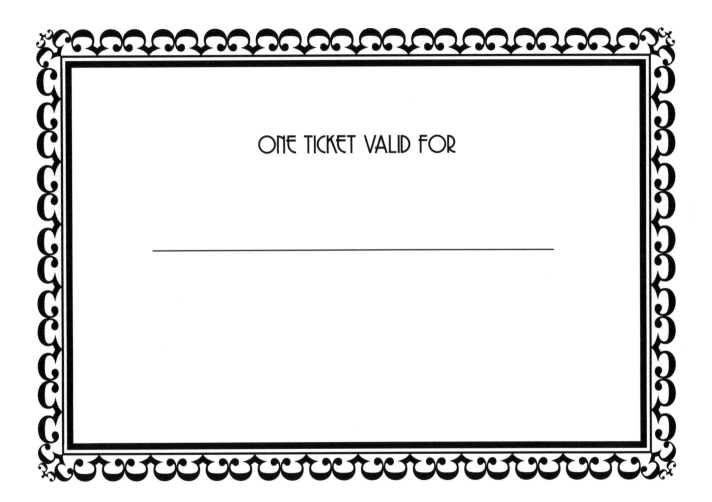

ONE TICKET VALID FOR

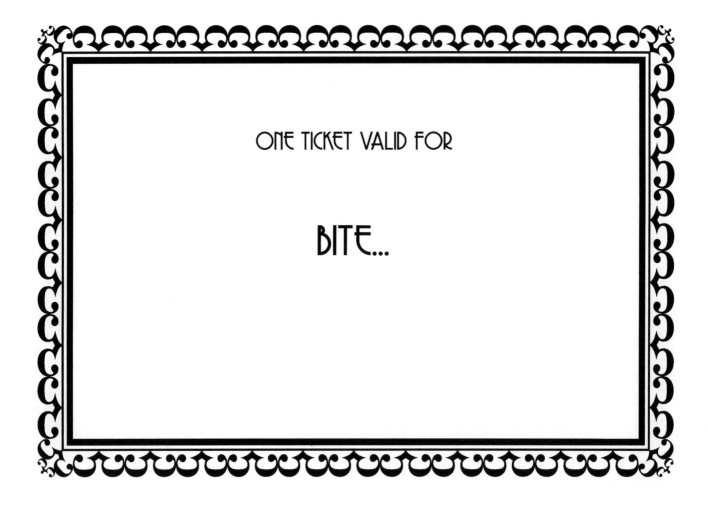

ONE TICKET VALID FOR

BITE...

ONE TICKET VALID FOR

ONE TICKET VALID FOR

HAVE SEX IN
A STRANGE LOCATION

ONE TICKET VALID FOR

_____

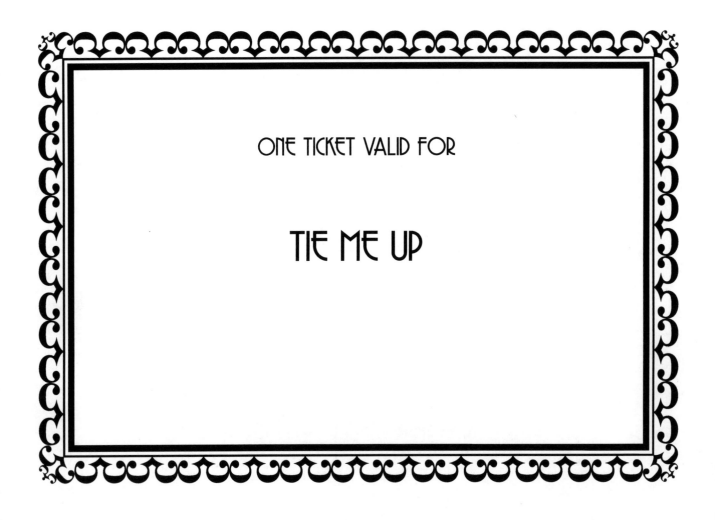

ONE TICKET VALID FOR

TIE ME UP

ONE TICKET VALID FOR

_____

ONE TICKET VALID FOR

ONE TICKET VALID FOR

PLAY SUB AND DOM
FOR ONCE

ONE TICKET VALID FOR

_____

ONE TICKET VALID FOR

_____

ONE TICKET VALID FOR

CUM ON HER LIPS

ONE TICKET VALID FOR

_____

ONE TICKET VALID FOR

KISS HER NECK AND
PLAY WITH HER BUTT

ONE TICKET VALID FOR

_____

ONE TICKET VALID FOR

_____

ONE TICKET VALID FOR

YOU PICK THE MUSIC
I PICK THE OUTFIT

ONE TICKET VALID FOR

_____

ONE TICKET VALID FOR

ROMANITC MEAL
AND SEX OVER THE TABLE

ONE TICKET VALID FOR

_____

ONE TICKET VALID FOR

EROTIC PHONE CALL

ONE TICKET VALID FOR

_____

ONE TICKET VALID FOR

MUTUAL MASTURBATION

ONE TICKET VALID FOR

_____

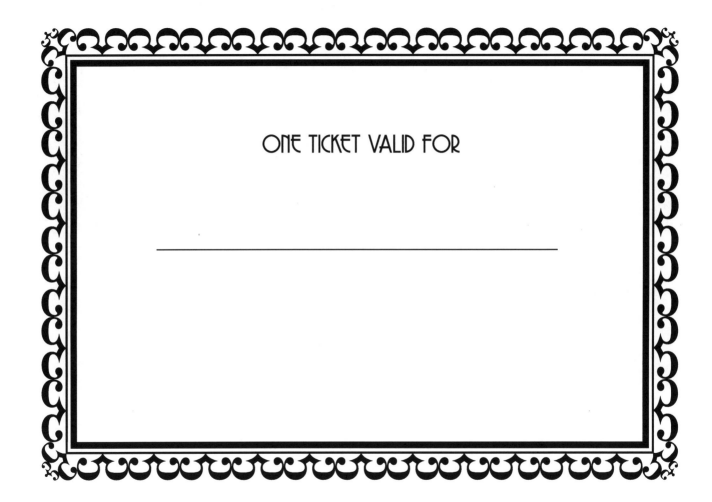

ONE TICKET VALID FOR

_____

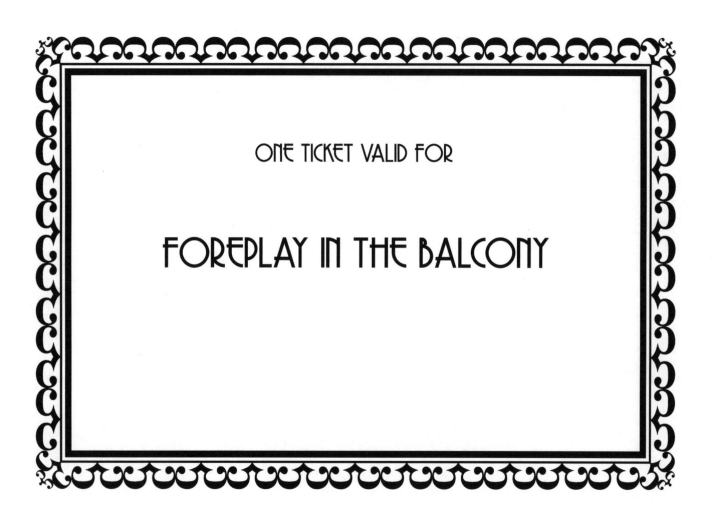

ONE TICKET VALID FOR

FOREPLAY IN THE BALCONY

ONE TICKET VALID FOR

_____

ONE TICKET VALID FOR

SKINNY DIP

ONE TICKET VALID FOR

_____

ONE TICKET VALID FOR

MAKE SEX BLINDFOLDED

ONE TICKET VALID FOR

_____

ONE TICKET VALID FOR

BREAKFAST IN BED
NAKED, PLAYING WITH
THE FOOD

ONE TICKET VALID FOR

_____

ONE TICKET VALID FOR

LIPSTICK, HEELS AND MINISKIRT!

ONE TICKET VALID FOR

_____

ONE TICKET VALID FOR

SEX IN THE CAR

ONE TICKET VALID FOR

_____

ONE TICKET VALID FOR

_____

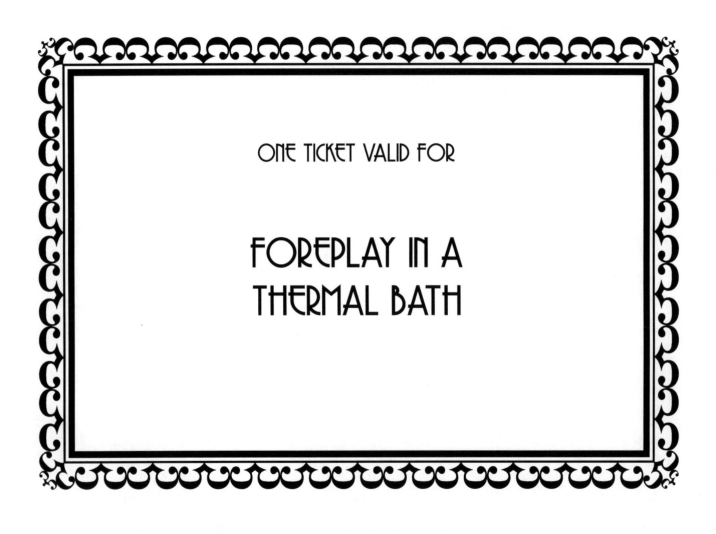

ONE TICKET VALID FOR

FOREPLAY IN A
THERMAL BATH

ONE TICKET VALID FOR

ONE TICKET VALID FOR

PORN MOVIE TOGETHER

ONE TICKET VALID FOR

_____

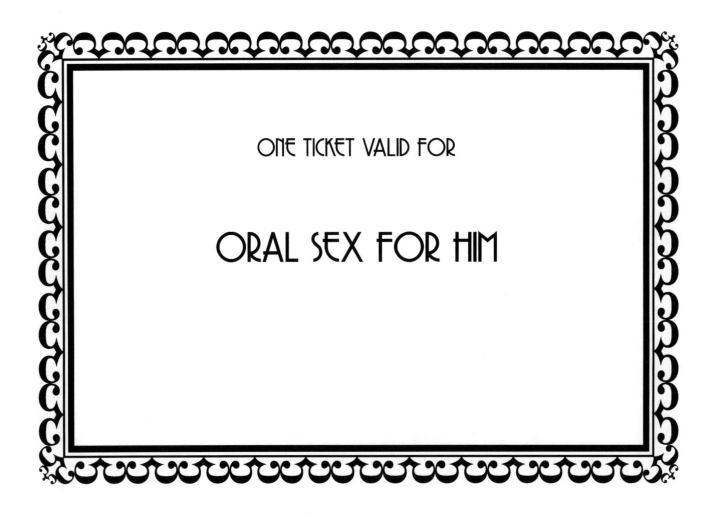

ONE TICKET VALID FOR

_____

ONE TICKET VALID FOR

SEX TOYS

ONE TICKET VALID FOR

_____

ONE TICKET VALID FOR

ONE TICKET VALID FOR

WAKE UP WITH
MORNING SEX

ONE TICKET VALID FOR

_____

ONE TICKET VALID FOR

READ AN EROTIC NOVEL

ONE TICKET VALID FOR

_____

ONE TICKET VALID FOR

SEX TAPE

ONE TICKET VALID FOR

_____

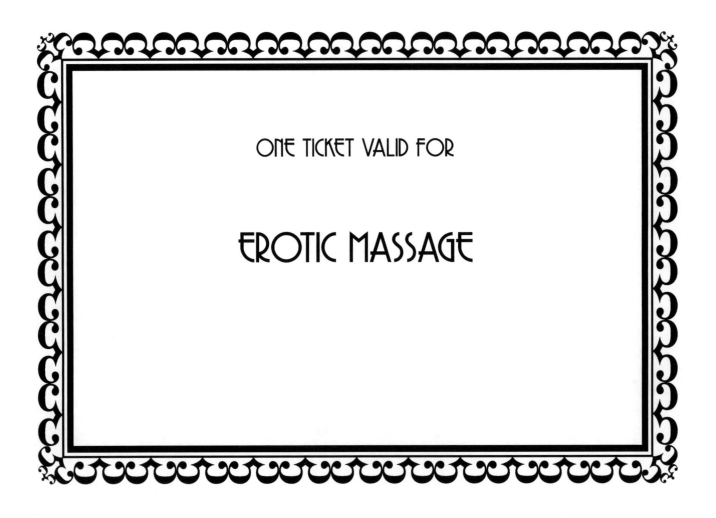

ONE TICKET VALID FOR

EROTIC MASSAGE

ONE TICKET VALID FOR

_____

ONE TICKET VALID FOR

_____

ONE TICKET VALID FOR

NAUGHTY FREE WISH

ONE TICKET VALID FOR

IF YOU LIKED THESE COUPONS,
BUT YOU WANT TO GIVE YOUR
DIRTY
CONTRIBUTE...
SEND AN EMAIL HERE:

DIANAMOONLCB@GMAIL.COM

WE WILL PERSONALLY MODIFY FUTURES BOOKS CONSIDERING YOUR TASTES!